From Dough to Delight: The Pierogi Cookbook

Coledown Kitchen

Published by Coledown Kitchen, 2023.

While every precaution has been taken in the preparation of this book, the publisher assumes no responsibility for errors or omissions, or for damages resulting from the use of the information contained herein.

FROM DOUGH TO DELIGHT: THE PIEROGI COOKBOOK

First edition. July 29, 2023.

ISBN: 979-8223324591

Written by Coledown Kitchen.

Table of Contents

Introduction

———

Imagine a delightful pillow of dough, gently cradling a scrumptious filling that bursts with flavors, from savory to sweet. This heavenly creation is none other than the beloved pierogi, a culinary treasure hailing from the heart of Eastern Europe. Bursting with history, culture, and tradition, pierogi have captured the hearts and taste buds of people across the globe, becoming a symbol of comfort, love, and celebration.

The Enigmatic Origins

The roots of pierogi extend deep into the rich soils of Eastern Europe, where the story of these tantalizing dumplings begins. Unraveling the exact origins of pierogi is like tracing a delightful dance through centuries of folklore and culinary heritage.

Historical accounts point to the early influence of Chinese dumplings, believed to have traversed the Silk Road, eventually reaching the region of Central Asia. As trade routes expanded, so did the culinary repertoire, with the exchange of ideas and ingredients resulting in culinary cross-pollination.

In the lands of present-day Poland, Ukraine, and Russia, pierogi started to take shape. The word "pierogi" itself is believed to have derived from the Old Slavic word "pirъ," meaning "feast." Thus, pierogi became synonymous with festive occasions and celebrations, creating an inseparable link between food and festivities.

From Rural Kitchens to Royal Tables

In the early days, pierogi were primarily a rural specialty, crafted by skilled hands in humble kitchens. Women, known as "babci" or grandmothers, passed down cherished family recipes from one generation to the next. These women were the custodians of culinary wisdom, and their deft hands ensured that pierogi remained a symbol of love and togetherness.

As time passed, pierogi found their way from rural settings to the palaces of kings and queens. The delicacy of these dumplings, combined with the versatility of fillings, made them a favorite at royal banquets. Monarchs and aristocrats were enchanted by the comforting taste and unique shapes of pierogi, leading to their popularity spreading across the nobility.

A Mosaic of Regional Delights

As pierogi traveled across Eastern Europe, they encountered a mosaic of regional influences, leading to a delightful array of flavors and techniques. Each region embraced its own unique twist on these dumplings, creating a rich tapestry of culinary diversity.

In Poland, the classic pierogi ruskie emerged, featuring a filling of creamy potatoes and farmer's cheese. Meanwhile, the Ukraine took pride in their varenyky, stuffed with sweet berries, cherries, or savory fillings like sauerkraut and meat. The Russian pelmeni, a distant cousin of pierogi, were smaller and often served with a dollop of sour cream.

The Pinnacle of Festivities

In Eastern European culture, pierogi became synonymous with celebrations and gatherings. From Christmas and Easter to weddings and birthdays, no festive table was complete without the presence of these pillowy delights. The act of making pierogi itself turned into a communal celebration, with family and friends coming together to share stories and laughter while shaping these culinary masterpieces.

During Christmas Eve, the Polish tradition of "Wigilia" sees a twelve-course meal where pierogi, known as "pierogi wigilijne," take center stage. These dumplings, filled with sauerkraut, mushrooms, or lentils, honor the tradition of abstaining from meat before the midnight feast.

A Global Sensation

With time, pierogi transcended geographical boundaries and captured the hearts of food enthusiasts around the world. Immigrants carried their cherished pierogi recipes to new lands, introducing them to the culinary scenes of North America, Australia, and beyond.

In the United States, cities like Pittsburgh, Pennsylvania, earned the title of "Pierogi Capital," boasting annual festivals dedicated to these dumplings. Similarly, in Canada, the city of Winnipeg celebrates the "Folklorama," a multicultural festival where visitors indulge in pierogi alongside various other cultural delicacies.

A Modern Twist

While pierogi remain deeply rooted in tradition, contemporary chefs and food enthusiasts have embraced their creativity to give these classic dumplings a modern twist. Fusion pierogi, featuring ingredients from diverse cuisines, have become a hit with adventurous foodies.

Pierogi in Popular Culture

Beyond their culinary fame, pierogi have left an indelible mark on popular culture. From folklore and literature to music and art, these dumplings have found their way into the hearts of artists and storytellers.

In Polish folklore, the character of "Pierogi King" plays a prominent role, embodying the essence of tradition and festivities. In literature, mentions of pierogi bring to life the nostalgia of cherished family gatherings and heartwarming moments.

A Love for Pierogi, Past and Present

Throughout the ages, pierogi have remained a symbol of love, comfort, and togetherness. Whether served at a rustic family dinner or an extravagant celebration, these dumplings continue to evoke feelings of joy and happiness.

As the world embraces its diverse culinary heritage, pierogi stand tall as an enduring symbol of cultural identity and the joy of breaking bread together. The dumplings that once graced the tables of Eastern Europe have evolved into an international sensation, bridging cultures and uniting people through their shared love for these pillowy delights.

Homemade Pierogi Dough

While store-bought pierogi dough is readily available, crafting your own homemade dough adds an extra layer of love and authenticity to your pierogi creations. Making pierogi dough from scratch allows you to savor the process and infuse your own personal touch into these delectable dumplings.

Serves 4

Ingredients:

- 2 cups all-purpose flour, plus extra for kneading and rolling

- 1/2 teaspoon salt

- 1 large egg

- 1/2 cup warm water

- 2 tablespoons vegetable oil

Instructions:

1. Prepare Your Work Surface. Ensure you have a clean and well-floured work surface ready for kneading and rolling out the dough. A large wooden board or clean countertop works perfectly for this purpose.

2. In a large mixing bowl, combine the all-purpose flour and salt. Create a well in the center of the dry ingredients to prepare for the wet ingredients.

3. Crack the egg into the well you created in the flour mixture. Add the warm water and vegetable oil to the same well.

4. Using a fork, gently whisk the wet ingredients together within the well, gradually incorporating the surrounding flour mixture until a sticky dough forms.

5. Transfer the sticky dough onto your floured work surface. Knead the dough for about 5-7 minutes until it becomes smooth, elastic, and no longer sticky. Add more flour to the surface as needed to prevent sticking.

6. Shape the kneaded dough into a ball and place it back in the mixing bowl. Cover the bowl with a clean kitchen towel and let the dough rest for at least 30 minutes. This resting period allows the gluten to relax, making the dough easier to roll out later.

7. After the resting period, divide the dough into four equal portions. Working with one portion at a time, keep the others covered to prevent drying. On a floured surface, roll out each portion into a thin sheet, about 1/8 inch thick.

8. Using a round cutter or the rim of a glass, cut out circles from the rolled-out dough. Aim for circles that are about 3 inches in diameter. Gather and re-roll any dough scraps to utilize as much dough as possible.

9.Place a spoonful of your desired pierogi filling (from any of the chapters) onto one side of each dough circle. Fold the other half over the filling, forming a half-moon shape.

10. Press the edges firmly to seal the pierogi, ensuring no filling escapes during cooking.

11. Bring a large pot of salted water to a boil. Carefully drop the pierogi into the boiling water, working in batches if needed. Cook the pierogi until they float to the surface, usually around 2-3 minutes. Use a slotted spoon to remove the cooked pierogi and set them aside.

12. Now that your homemade pierogi are cooked and ready, it's time to serve and enjoy these delightful creations. You can opt for a simple garnish of melted butter, or choose to get creative with a variety of dipping sauces and toppings.

Chapter 1: The Classics

In this first chapter, we dive into the heart of pierogi goodness with a collection of traditional fillings that have stood the test of time. Each recipe in this chapter pays homage to the rich heritage of pierogi while adding a modern twist to elevate your culinary experience. S

Potato and Cheese Pierogi

Indulge in the ultimate comfort food - Potato and Cheese Pierogi! Imagine a cloud of fluffy mashed potatoes mingling with the tangy embrace of cheddar cheese and the fragrance of fresh herbs. All of this goodness is tucked lovingly inside a tender dough, waiting to melt in your mouth.

Serves Four

Ingredients:

- 2 cups mashed potatoes

- 1 cup shredded cheddar cheese

- 1 tablespoon fresh chives, finely chopped

- Salt and pepper, to taste

- Pierogi dough (store-bought or homemade)

Instructions:

1. In a bowl, combine the mashed potatoes, shredded cheddar cheese, and chopped chives. Season with salt and pepper to your liking. Mix well until the filling is smooth and well-combined.

2. Roll out the pierogi dough on a lightly floured surface. Use a round cutter or a glass to cut circles about 3 inches in diameter.

3. Place a spoonful of the potato and cheese filling in the center of each dough circle.

4. Fold the dough over the filling, forming a half-moon shape. Press the edges firmly to seal the pierogi.

5. Bring a large pot of salted water to a boil. Carefully drop the pierogi into the boiling water and cook until they float to the surface, about 2-3 minutes. Remove with a slotted spoon and set aside.

6. Serve hot with a dollop of sour cream or melted butter, and sprinkle some extra chives on top for a touch of freshness.

Spinach and Feta Fusion Pierogi

A match made in culinary heaven - Spinach and Feta Fusion Pierogi! Sauteed spinach joins forces with crumbled feta cheese, and a hint of zesty lemon zest, all wrapped up in a delicate pierogi.

Serves Four

Ingredients:

- 2 cups fresh spinach, chopped

- 1/2 cup crumbled feta cheese

- 1 teaspoon lemon zest

- Salt and pepper, to taste

- Pierogi dough (store-bought or homemade)

Instructions:

1. In a pan, sauté the chopped spinach until wilted. Season with salt and pepper to taste. Remove from heat and let it cool slightly.

2. In a bowl, combine the sautéed spinach, crumbled feta cheese, and lemon zest. Mix well to evenly distribute the flavors.

3. Roll out the pierogi dough and cut out circles about 3 inches in diameter.

4. Place a spoonful of the spinach and feta filling in the center of each dough circle.

5. Fold the dough over the filling, sealing the pierogi by pressing the edges firmly.

6. Bring a large pot of salted water to a boil. Add the pierogi and cook until they float to the surface, about 2-3 minutes. Remove with a slotted spoon and set aside.

7. Serve hot with a drizzle of olive oil or a sprinkle of lemon zest for an extra citrusy kick.

Sweet Onion and Mushroom Medley Pierogi

Caramelized onions, savory mushrooms, and a touch of thyme unite to create a pierogi that embraces you like a warm hug on a chilly day. Savor each bite and let the flavors take you on a journey of pure contentment!

Serves Four

Ingredients:

- 2 cups onions, thinly sliced

- 1 ½ cups mushrooms, sliced

- 1 teaspoon fresh thyme leaves

- 2 tablespoons butter

- Salt and pepper, to taste

- Pierogi dough (store-bought or homemade)

Instructions:

1. In a pan, melt the butter over medium heat. Add the sliced onions and cook until caramelized, stirring occasionally for about 15-20 minutes.

2. Add the sliced mushrooms to the pan and cook until they become tender and lightly browned. Season with salt, pepper, and fresh thyme leaves.

3. Roll out the pierogi dough and cut out circles about 3 inches in diameter.

4. Place a spoonful of the sweet onion and mushroom filling in the center of each dough circle.

5. Fold the dough over the filling, sealing the pierogi by pressing the edges firmly.

6. Bring a large pot of salted water to a boil. Add the pierogi and cook until they float to the surface, about 2-3 minutes. Remove with a slotted spoon and set aside.

7. Serve hot with a dollop of sour cream or a sprinkle of fresh thyme leaves for a fragrant finishing touch.

Bacon and Caramelized Shallots Pierogi

Prepare your taste buds for a flavor explosion with Bacon and Caramelized Shallots Pierogi! The rich smokiness of bacon combines with the sweetness of caramelized shallots to create a tantalizing filling.

Serves Four

Ingredients:

- 1 cup bacon, cooked and crumbled

- 1 cup shallots, thinly sliced

- 2 tablespoons butter

- Salt and pepper, to taste

- Pierogi dough (store-bought or homemade)

Instructions:

1. In a pan, melt the butter over medium heat. Add the sliced shallots and cook until they become soft and caramelized, about 10-12 minutes.

2. Add the crumbled bacon to the pan and cook for an additional 2-3 minutes, allowing the flavors to meld. Season with salt and pepper to taste.

3. Roll out the pierogi dough and cut out circles about 3 inches in diameter.

4. Place a spoonful of the bacon and caramelized shallot filling in the center of each dough circle.

5. Fold the dough over the filling, sealing the pierogi by pressing the edges firmly.

6. Bring a large pot of salted water to a boil. Add the pierogi and cook until they float to the surface, about 2-3 minutes. Remove with a slotted spoon and set aside.

7. Serve hot with a sprinkle of fresh ground black pepper for an extra kick of flavor.

Classic Sauerkraut Delight Pierogi

A pierogi classic that never disappoints - Classic Sauerkraut Delight! Embrace the tangy goodness of sauerkraut filling with hints of caraway seeds, perfectly balanced to take you on a nostalgic journey to old-world flavors.

Serves Four

Ingredients:

- 2 cups sauerkraut, drained and rinsed

- 1 tablespoon butter

- 1 teaspoon caraway seeds

- Salt and pepper, to taste

- Pierogi dough (store-bought or homemade)

Instructions:

1. In a pan, melt the butter over medium heat. Add the drained sauerkraut and caraway seeds.

2. Cook the sauerkraut for about 5-7 minutes, allowing the flavors to meld. Season with salt and pepper to taste.

3. Roll out the pierogi dough and cut out circles about 3 inches in diameter.

4. Place a spoonful of the sauerkraut filling in the center of each dough circle.

5. Fold the dough over the filling, sealing the pierogi by pressing the edges firmly.

6. Bring a large pot of salted water to a boil. Add the pierogi and cook until they float to the surface, about 2-3 minutes. Remove with a slotted spoon and set aside.

7. Serve hot with a dollop of sour cream and a sprinkle of caraway seeds for an authentic touch.

Chapter 2: International Fusion

———

Prepare your taste buds for a thrilling global tour as we bring you pierogi recipes inspired by the diverse and vibrant cuisines of the world. These international twists will take your pierogi experience to a whole new level, transporting you to the culinary corners of Mexico, the Mediterranean, India, Japan, and Thailand.

Mexican Fiesta Pierogi

Get ready for a fiesta in your mouth with our Mexican Fiesta Pierogi! These little pockets of joy are packed with a zesty punch of spicy ground beef, hearty black beans, and a generous ooze of melted cheese. Serves Four

Ingredients:

- 1/2 lb ground beef

- 1 cup black beans, cooked and drained

- 1 cup shredded Mexican blend cheese

- 1 teaspoon chili powder

- 1/2 teaspoon cumin

- Salt and pepper, to taste

- Pierogi dough (store-bought or homemade)

Instructions:

1. In a skillet over medium heat, brown the ground beef, breaking it into crumbles as it cooks. Drain any excess fat.

2. Add the cooked black beans, shredded Mexican cheese blend, chili powder, cumin, salt, and pepper to the skillet with the beef. Mix well until the filling is well-combined and the cheese is melted.

3. Roll out the pierogi dough on a lightly floured surface. Cut circles about 3 inches in diameter.

4. Place a spoonful of the Mexican fiesta filling in the center of each dough circle.

5. Fold the dough over the filling, forming a half-moon shape. Press the edges firmly to seal the pierogi.

6. Bring a large pot of salted water to a boil. Carefully drop the pierogi into the boiling water and cook until they float to the surface, about 2-3 minutes. Remove with a slotted spoon and set aside.

7. Serve hot with a dollop of guacamole, a drizzle of sour cream, and a sprinkle of chopped cilantro for that perfect fiesta flair!

Mediterranean Magic Pierogi

Take your taste buds on a trip to the sun-soaked shores of the Mediterranean with our Mediterranean Magic Pierogi! Sundried tomatoes, briny olives, and crumbled feta cheese blend together in perfect harmony.

Serves Four

Ingredients:

- 1/2 cup sundried tomatoes, rehydrated and chopped

- 1/2 cup Kalamata olives, pitted and chopped

- 1 cup crumbled feta cheese

- 1 tablespoon fresh basil, finely chopped

- Pierogi dough (store-bought or homemade)

Instructions:

1. In a bowl, combine the rehydrated and chopped sundried tomatoes, Kalamata olives, crumbled feta cheese, and chopped fresh basil. Mix well to distribute the flavors evenly.

2. Roll out the pierogi dough and cut out circles about 3 inches in diameter.

3. Place a spoonful of the Mediterranean magic filling in the center of each dough circle.

4. Fold the dough over the filling, sealing the pierogi by pressing the edges firmly.

5. Bring a large pot of salted water to a boil. Add the pierogi and cook until they float to the surface, about 2-3 minutes. Remove with a slotted spoon and set aside.

6. Serve hot with a drizzle of extra virgin olive oil and a sprinkle of freshly ground black pepper for a taste of the Mediterranean breeze!

Indian Spice Pierogi

These little parcels are bursting with flavor, featuring a curry-infused filling of tender potatoes, sweet peas, and aromatic spices. Each bite is a celebration of exotic tastes that will awaken your senses!

Serves Four

Ingredients:

- 2 cups potatoes, boiled and mashed

- 1 cup green peas, cooked

- 1 tablespoon vegetable oil

- 1 teaspoon cumin seeds

- 1 teaspoon ground coriander

- 1/2 teaspoon turmeric

- 1/2 teaspoon garam masala

- Salt, to taste

- Pierogi dough (store-bought or homemade)

Instructions:

1. In a pan, heat the vegetable oil over medium heat. Add the cumin seeds and let them sizzle for a few seconds until fragrant.

2. Add the boiled and mashed potatoes, cooked green peas, ground coriander, turmeric, garam masala, and salt to the pan. Mix well until the filling is infused with the aromatic spices. Cook for a couple of minutes to allow the flavors to meld.

3. Roll out the pierogi dough and cut out circles about 3 inches in diameter.

4. Place a spoonful of the Indian spice filling in the center of each dough circle.

5. Fold the dough over the filling, sealing the pierogi by pressing the edges firmly.

6. Bring a large pot of salted water to a boil. Add the pierogi and cook until they float to the surface, about 2-3 minutes. Remove with a slotted spoon and set aside.

7. Serve hot with a dollop of cooling cucumber raita or tangy tamarind chutney to balance the flavors.

Japanese Gyoza-inspired Pierogi

Ground pork meets the flavors of ginger and garlic, all wrapped in a tender pierogi dough. Serve these dumplings with a soy-vinegar dipping sauce for a taste of Japan!

Serves Four

Ingredients:

- 1/2 lb ground pork

- 2 tablespoons soy sauce

- 1 tablespoon sesame oil

- 1 tablespoon fresh ginger, minced

- 2 cloves garlic, minced

- 1 cup cabbage, finely shredded

- Salt and pepper, to taste

- Pierogi dough (store-bought or homemade)

Instructions:

1. In a bowl, combine the ground pork, soy sauce, sesame oil, minced ginger, and minced garlic. Mix well to incorporate the flavors.

2. Add the finely shredded cabbage to the bowl and mix it into the pork mixture. Season with salt and pepper to taste.

3. Roll out the pierogi dough on a lightly floured surface. Cut circles about 3 inches in diameter.

4. Place a spoonful of the Japanese gyoza filling in the center of each dough circle.

5. Fold the dough over the filling, forming a half-moon shape. Press the edges firmly to seal the pierogi.

6. Bring a large pot of salted water to a boil. Carefully drop the pierogi into the boiling water and cook until they float to the surface, about 2-3 minutes. Remove with a slotted spoon and set aside.

7. Serve hot with a soy-vinegar dipping sauce for an authentic Japanese experience. Combine soy sauce, rice vinegar, a splash of sesame oil, and a pinch of red pepper flakes for a perfect dipping sauce!

Thai Coconut Curry Delight Pierogi

Prepare for a burst of flavors that will transport you to the vibrant streets of Thailand! Creamy coconut milk, aromatic red curry, and succulent shrimp come together to create an enchanting taste sensation.

Serves Four

Ingredients:

- 1/2 lb shrimp, peeled and deveined

- 1 can (13.5 oz) coconut milk

- 2 tablespoons Thai red curry paste

- 1 tablespoon fish sauce

- 1 tablespoon brown sugar

- Fresh cilantro leaves, for garnish

- Pierogi dough (store-bought or homemade)

Instructions:

1. In a pan, cook the shrimp until they turn pink and are cooked through. Set them aside.

2. In the same pan, add the Thai red curry paste and sauté for a minute until fragrant.

3. Pour in the coconut milk, fish sauce, and brown sugar. Stir well to combine the flavors, allowing the sauce to thicken slightly.

4. Add the cooked shrimp back into the sauce, mixing them to coat in the flavorful curry sauce.

5. Roll out the pierogi dough and cut out circles about 3 inches in diameter.

6. Place a spoonful of the Thai coconut curry filling in the center of each dough circle.

7. Fold the dough over the filling, sealing the pierogi by pressing the edges firmly.

8. Bring a large pot of salted water to a boil. Add the pierogi and cook until they float to the surface, about 2-3 minutes. Remove with a slotted spoon and set aside.

9. Serve hot with a garnish of fresh cilantro leaves and a side of jasmine rice for the complete Thai dining experience!

Chapter 3: Vegetable Extravaganza

———

Get ready to revel in a celebration of fresh and flavorful vegetables as we present a delightful assortment of vegetarian pierogi. Each recipe in this chapter is a testament to the incredible versatility of vegetables, transformed into velvety fillings and scrumptious combinations that will satisfy every palate.

Roasted Butternut Squash Pierogi

Roasted butternut squash takes center stage, mingling with the sweetness of caramelized onions and the fragrant embrace of sage. This velvety filling is wrapped lovingly in a tender pierogi dough, creating a dish that exudes comfort and warmth with every bite.

Serves Four

Ingredients:

- 2 cups roasted butternut squash, mashed

- 1 cup caramelized onions

- 1 tablespoon fresh sage leaves, finely chopped

- Salt and pepper, to taste

- Pierogi dough (store-bought or homemade)

Instructions:

1. In a bowl, combine the mashed roasted butternut squash, caramelized onions, and chopped fresh sage leaves. Season with salt and pepper to your liking. Mix well until the filling is smooth and well-combined.

2. Roll out the pierogi dough on a lightly floured surface. Use a round cutter or a glass to cut circles about 3 inches in diameter.

3. Place a spoonful of the roasted butternut squash filling in the center of each dough circle.

4. Fold the dough over the filling, forming a half-moon shape. Press the edges firmly to seal the pierogi.

5. Bring a large pot of salted water to a boil. Carefully drop the pierogi into the boiling water and cook until they float to the surface, about 2-3 minutes. Remove with a slotted spoon and set aside.

6. Serve hot with a sprinkle of chopped sage leaves and a drizzle of melted butter.

Broccoli and Cheddar Pierogi

Nutritious broccoli florets meet gooey cheddar cheese to create a delightful filling that will satisfy both your taste buds and your health-conscious side.

Serves Four

Ingredients:

- 2 cups broccoli florets, steamed and chopped

- 1 cup shredded cheddar cheese

- 1 teaspoon garlic powder

- Salt and pepper, to taste

- Pierogi dough (store-bought or homemade)

Instructions:

1. In a bowl, combine the chopped steamed broccoli florets, shredded cheddar cheese, garlic powder, salt, and pepper. Mix well until the filling is evenly combined and the cheese is melted.

2. Roll out the pierogi dough and cut out circles about 3 inches in diameter.

3. Place a spoonful of the broccoli and cheddar filling in the center of each dough circle.

4. Fold the dough over the filling, sealing the pierogi by pressing the edges firmly.

5. Bring a large pot of salted water to a boil. Add the pierogi and cook until they float to the surface, about 2-3 minutes. Remove with a slotted spoon and set aside.

6. Serve hot with a sprinkle of freshly ground black pepper for an extra kick of flavor.

Creamy Avocado and Lime Fiesta Pierogi

Indulge in the creamy richness of mashed avocado, the zesty tang of lime juice, and the vibrant freshness of cilantro.

Serves Four

Ingredients:

- 2 ripe avocados, mashed

- 2 tablespoons fresh lime juice

- 1 tablespoon fresh cilantro, finely chopped

- Salt and pepper, to taste

- Pierogi dough (store-bought or homemade)

Instructions:

1. In a bowl, mash the ripe avocados until smooth and creamy.

2. Add the fresh lime juice, finely chopped cilantro, salt, and pepper to the bowl. Mix well to create a zesty avocado filling.

3. Roll out the pierogi dough and cut out circles about 3 inches in diameter.

4. Place a spoonful of the creamy avocado and lime filling in the center of each dough circle.

5. Fold the dough over the filling, sealing the pierogi by pressing the edges firmly.

6. Bring a large pot of salted water to a boil. Add the pierogi and cook until they float to the surface, about 2-3 minutes. Remove with a slotted spoon and set aside.

7. Serve hot with a garnish of fresh cilantro leaves and a squeeze of lime for an extra fiesta flavor!

Caprese Pierogi

Transport yourself to the heart of Italy! Juicy cherry tomatoes, aromatic fresh basil, and creamy mozzarella cheese come together in a mouthwatering embrace. Drizzled with balsamic glaze, this pierogi version of the Italian classic will whisk you away to a Mediterranean dream!

Serves Four

Ingredients:

- 1 cup cherry tomatoes, halved

- 1/2 cup fresh basil leaves, torn

- 1 cup fresh mozzarella, cubed

- Balsamic glaze, for drizzling

- Pierogi dough (store-bought or homemade)

Instructions:

1. In a bowl, combine the halved cherry tomatoes, torn fresh basil leaves, and cubed fresh mozzarella. Mix gently to preserve the shape of the ingredients.

2. Roll out the pierogi dough and cut out circles about 3 inches in diameter.

3. Place a spoonful of the Caprese filling in the center of each dough circle.

4. Fold the dough over the filling, sealing the pierogi by pressing the edges firmly.

5. Bring a large pot of salted water to a boil. Add the pierogi and cook until they float to the surface, about 2-3 minutes. Remove with a slotted spoon and set aside.

6. Serve hot with a drizzle of balsamic glaze.

Savory Beetroot Pierogi

Earthy roasted beets are paired with creamy goat cheese and crunchy toasted walnuts to create a filling that's as delightful to the eyes as it is to the taste buds.

Serves Four

Ingredients:

- 2 cups roasted beets, diced

- 1/2 cup goat cheese, crumbled

- 1/4 cup toasted walnuts, chopped

- Salt and pepper, to taste

- Pierogi dough (store-bought or homemade)

Instructions:

1. In a bowl, combine the diced roasted beets, crumbled goat cheese, and chopped toasted walnuts. Mix gently to keep the colors and textures intact.

2. Roll out

the pierogi dough and cut out circles about 3 inches in diameter.

3. Place a spoonful of the savory beetroot filling in the center of each dough circle.

4. Fold the dough over the filling, sealing the pierogi by pressing the edges firmly.

5. Bring a large pot of salted water to a boil. Add the pierogi and cook until they float to the surface, about 2-3 minutes. Remove with a slotted spoon and set aside.

6. Serve hot with a sprinkle of fresh ground black pepper for an extra touch of flavor.

Chapter 4: Decadent Desserts

———

Prepare to indulge your sweet tooth as we take you on a journey of pure dessert bliss. These delightful pierogi recipes will satisfy your cravings for all things decadent and sweet.

Chocolate Lover's Dream Pierogi

Calling all chocolate lovers! Decadent dark chocolate and hazelnut filling take center stage, crowned with a drizzle of luxurious chocolate sauce.

Serves Four

Ingredients:

- 1 cup dark chocolate chips

- 1/2 cup hazelnut spread

- 1/4 cup heavy cream

- Pierogi dough (store-bought or homemade)

Instructions:

1. In a microwave-safe bowl, melt the dark chocolate chips in short intervals, stirring in between until smooth and melted.

2. Stir in the hazelnut spread until fully combined, creating a luscious chocolate-hazelnut filling.

3. Roll out the pierogi dough on a lightly floured surface. Cut circles about 3 inches in diameter.

4. Place a spoonful of the chocolate-hazelnut filling in the center of each dough circle.

5. Fold the dough over the filling, forming a half-moon shape. Press the edges firmly to seal the pierogi.

6. Bring a large pot of water to a gentle simmer. Carefully drop the pierogi into the simmering water and cook for about 3-4 minutes until they float to the surface. Remove with a slotted spoon and set aside.

7. Serve hot with a drizzle of rich chocolate sauce over the top for an indulgent finish.

Apple Pie Pierogi

Cinnamon-spiced apples and brown sugar create a comforting filling that brings the essence of apple pie to your pierogi plate. Top it off with a dollop of creamy vanilla ice cream for the ultimate dessert delight!

Serves Four

Ingredients:

- 2 cups apples, peeled and diced

- 2 tablespoons butter

- 1/4 cup brown sugar

- 1 teaspoon ground cinnamon

- Vanilla ice cream, for serving

- Pierogi dough (store-bought or homemade)

Instructions:

1. In a pan, melt the butter over medium heat. Add the diced apples, brown sugar, and ground cinnamon. Cook until the apples are tender and coated in the sweet and spicy mixture.

2. Roll out the pierogi dough and cut out circles about 3 inches in diameter.

3. Place a spoonful of the apple filling in the center of each dough circle.

4. Fold the dough over the filling, forming a half-moon shape. Press the edges firmly to seal the pierogi.

5. Bring a large pot of water to a gentle simmer. Carefully drop the pierogi into the simmering water and cook for about 3-4 minutes until they float to the surface. Remove with a slotted spoon and set aside.

6. Serve hot with a scoop of creamy vanilla ice cream on top for the perfect apple pie-inspired treat.

Strawberry Cheesecake Pierogi

A creamy blend of strawberries and cream cheese awaits inside each pierogi, topped with a sprinkle of graham cracker crumbs for added delight.

Serves Four

Ingredients:

- 1 cup strawberries, finely chopped

- 4 ounces cream cheese, softened

- 1/4 cup powdered sugar

- 1 teaspoon vanilla extract

- Crushed graham cracker crumbs, for garnish

- Pierogi dough (store-bought or homemade)

Instructions:

1. In a bowl, combine the finely chopped strawberries, softened cream cheese, powdered sugar, and vanilla extract. Mix until the filling is smooth and well-combined, creating a delectable cheesecake filling.

2. Roll out the pierogi dough and cut out circles about 3 inches in diameter.

3. Place a spoonful of the strawberry cheesecake filling in the center of each dough circle.

4. Fold the dough over the filling, forming a half-moon shape. Press the edges firmly to seal the pierogi.

5. Bring a large pot of water to a gentle simmer. Carefully drop the pierogi into the simmering water and cook for about 3-4 minutes until they float to the surface. Remove with a slotted spoon and set aside.

6. Serve hot with a sprinkle of crushed graham cracker crumbs over the top for a delightful touch of cheesecake bliss!

Bananas Foster Pierogi

Embrace the flavors of New Orleans with our Bananas Foster Pierogi! Caramelized bananas, brown sugar, and a splash of rum come together to create an irresistible dessert delight.

Serves Four

Ingredients:

- 2 ripe bananas, sliced

- 1/4 cup unsalted butter

- 1/4 cup brown sugar

- 2 tablespoons rum (optional)

- Whipped cream, for serving

- Pierogi dough (store-bought or homemade)

Instructions:

1. In a pan, melt the unsalted butter over medium heat. Add the sliced bananas, brown sugar, and rum (if using). Cook until the bananas are caramelized and coated in the delicious buttery sauce.

2. Roll out the pierogi dough and cut out circles about 3 inches in diameter.

3. Place a spoonful of the bananas foster filling in the center of each dough circle.

4. Fold the dough over the filling, forming a half-moon shape. Press the edges firmly to seal the pierogi.

5. Bring a large pot of water to a gentle simmer. Carefully drop the pierogi into the simmering water and cook for about 3-4 minutes until they float to the surface. Remove with a slotted spoon and set aside.

6. Serve hot with a dollop of whipped cream.

Lemon Blueberry Pierogi

Zesty lemon-infused blueberries take the spotlight in our Lemon Blueberry Pierogi! This sweet and tangy combination is wrapped inside a delicate pierogi dough and topped with a sprinkle of powdered sugar. Get ready for a burst of refreshing flavors in this delightful dessert treat!

Serves Four

Ingredients:

- 2 cups blueberries

- Zest of 1 lemon

- 2 tablespoons lemon juice

- 1/4 cup granulated sugar

- Powdered sugar, for garnish

- Pierogi dough (store-bought or homemade)

Instructions:

1. In a bowl, combine the blueberries, lemon zest, lemon juice, and granulated sugar. Mix well, allowing the flavors to meld and create a sweet and tangy blueberry delight.

2. Roll out the pierogi dough and cut out circles about 3 inches in diameter.

3. Place a spoonful of the lemon blueberry filling in the center of each dough circle.

4. Fold the dough over the filling, forming a half-moon shape. Press the edges firmly to seal the pierogi.

5. Bring a large pot of water to a gentle simmer. Carefully drop the pierogi into the simmering water and cook for about 3-4 minutes until they float to the surface. Remove with a slotted spoon and set aside.

6. Serve hot with a sprinkle of powdered sugar on top for a refreshing Lemon Blueberry Delight that's perfect for any sunny day!

Chapter 9: Seafood Sensations

———

Seafood pierogi, a delightful fusion of land and sea, offer a tantalizing array of flavors that are sure to impress even the most discerning palates. From succulent shrimp to tender crabmeat, let's dive into the world of Seafood Sensations!

Creamy Shrimp Scampi Pierogi

Indulge in the luxuriously creamy flavors of our Shrimp Scampi Pierogi, where succulent shrimp takes the spotlight, harmoniously mingling with garlic, butter, and a splash of white wine. This seafood twist on a classic Italian dish will transport you to the coastal shores of Italy in every delectable bite.

Serves Four

Ingredients:

- 1 lb large shrimp, peeled and deveined

- 4 tablespoons unsalted butter

- 4 garlic cloves, minced

- 1/4 cup white wine

- 1/4 cup heavy cream

- Fresh parsley, chopped, for garnish

- Pierogi dough (store-bought or homemade)

Instructions:

1. In a pan, melt 2 tablespoons of butter over medium heat. Add the minced garlic and sauté until fragrant, about 1 minute.

2. Add the peeled and deveined shrimp to the pan, cooking until they turn pink and are cooked through. Set them aside.

3. In the same pan, add the white wine and bring to a simmer, allowing it to reduce slightly.

4. Lower the heat and stir in the heavy cream and the remaining 2 tablespoons of butter. Cook until the sauce thickens slightly.

5. Roll out the pierogi dough and cut out circles about 3 inches in diameter.

6. Place a spoonful of the creamy shrimp scampi filling in the center of each dough circle.

7. Fold the dough over the filling, forming a half-moon shape. Press the edges firmly to seal the pierogi.

8. Bring a large pot of salted water to a boil. Carefully drop the pierogi into the boiling water and cook until they float to the surface, about 2-3 minutes. Remove with a slotted spoon and set aside.

9. Serve hot with a sprinkle of freshly chopped parsley for a burst of color and a taste of the sea!

Lobster and Corn Pierogi

Elevate your pierogi experience with our Lobster and Corn Pierogi, where succulent lobster meat meets sweet corn in a harmonious celebration of flavors. This luxurious seafood pierogi is a culinary masterpiece that will leave your taste buds longing for more.

Serves Four

Ingredients:

- 1 lb cooked lobster meat, chopped

- 1 cup corn kernels, fresh or frozen

- 2 tablespoons unsalted butter

- 1/4 cup heavy cream

- Fresh chives, chopped, for garnish

- Pierogi dough (store-bought or homemade)

Instructions:

1. In a pan, melt the unsalted butter over medium heat. Add the corn kernels and sauté until they become tender and slightly golden.

2. Stir in the chopped lobster meat and cook for a few minutes until heated through.

3. Lower the heat and pour in the heavy cream, stirring gently until the sauce becomes creamy and coats the lobster and corn mixture.

4. Roll out the pierogi dough and cut out circles about 3 inches in diameter.

5. Place a spoonful of the lobster and corn filling in the center of each dough circle.

6. Fold the dough over the filling, forming a half-moon shape. Press the edges firmly to seal the pierogi.

7. Bring a large pot of salted water to a boil. Add the pierogi and cook until they float to the surface, about 2-3 minutes. Remove with a slotted spoon and set aside.

8. Serve hot with a garnish of freshly chopped chives for an elegant touch to your seafood indulgence!

Smoked Salmon and Dill Pierogi

Embrace the delicate flavors of our Smoked Salmon and Dill Pierogi, where the distinct smokiness of salmon meets the refreshing notes of dill.

Serves Four

Ingredients:

- 1 cup smoked salmon, chopped

- 2 tablespoons fresh dill, chopped

- 1/4 cup cream cheese

- Lemon wedges, for serving

- Pierogi dough (store-bought or homemade)

Instructions:

1. In a bowl, combine the chopped smoked salmon, fresh dill, and cream cheese. Mix until well-combined, creating a creamy filling that celebrates the flavors of the sea.

2. Roll out the pierogi dough and cut out circles about 3 inches in diameter.

3. Place a spoonful of the smoked salmon and dill filling in the center of each dough circle.

4. Fold the dough over the filling, forming a half-moon shape. Press the edges firmly to seal the pierogi.

5. Bring a large pot of salted water to a boil. Carefully drop the pierogi into the boiling water and cook until they float to the surface, about 2-3 minutes. Remove with a slotted spoon and set aside.

6. Serve hot with a squeeze of fresh lemon juice for a zesty enhancement to the delicate smoked salmon flavors.

Crab and Avocado Pierogi

Indulge in the tantalizing flavors of our Crab and Avocado Pierogi, where tender crabmeat meets the creamy richness of avocado. This seafood fusion is a symphony of textures and flavors that will transport you to a beachside paradise with each mouthwatering bite.

Serves Four

Ingredients:

- 1 cup cooked crabmeat, flaked

- 2 ripe avocados, mashed

- 1 tablespoon lime juice

- 1 tablespoon fresh cilantro, chopped

- Pierogi dough (store-bought or homemade)

Instructions:

1. In a bowl, combine the flaked crabmeat, mashed avocados, lime juice, and fresh cilantro. Mix until the filling is well-combined and the flavors have melded.

2. Roll out the pierogi dough and cut out circles about 3 inches in diameter.

3. Place a spoonful of the crab and avocado filling in the center of each dough circle.

4. Fold the dough over the filling, forming a half-moon shape. Press the edges firmly to seal the pierogi.

5. Bring a large pot of salted water to a boil. Add the pierogi and cook until they float to the surface, about 2-3 minutes. Remove with a slotted spoon and set aside.

6. Serve hot with a sprinkle of fresh cilantro for a burst of color.

Spicy Tuna Pierogi

Prepare for a spicy dance of flavors with our Spicy Tuna Pierogi, where fiery tuna meets tangy lime and zesty spices.

Serves Four

Ingredients:

- 1 cup canned tuna, drained and flaked

- 2 tablespoons mayonnaise

- 1 tablespoon Sriracha sauce (adjust to your preferred spice level)

- 1 tablespoon lime juice

- Fresh cilantro, for garnish

- Pierogi dough (store-bought or homemade)

Instructions:

1. In a bowl, combine the flaked tuna, mayonnaise, Sriracha sauce, and lime juice. Mix until the filling is well-coated and the spicy tuna flavors have melded together.

2. Roll out the pierogi dough and cut out circles about 3 inches in diameter.

3. Place a spoonful of the spicy tuna filling in the center of each dough circle.

4. Fold the dough over the filling, forming a half-moon shape. Press the edges firmly to seal the pierogi.

5. Bring a large pot of salted water to a boil. Carefully drop the pierogi into the boiling water and cook until they float to the surface, about 2-3 minutes. Remove with a slotted spoon and set aside.

6. Serve hot with a garnish of fresh cilantro for a burst of color and an extra kick of flavor.

Chapter 9: Savory Meat Pierogi

———

In this chapter, we celebrate the hearty and flavorful world of meat pierogi, where succulent fillings and aromatic spices combine to create a truly satisfying culinary experience. From tender beef and savory pork to flavorful chicken and indulgent lamb, meat pierogi offer a diverse range of tastes to please every palate.

Classic Beef and Onion Pierogi

Our Classic Beef and Onion Pierogi is a timeless favorite that will have you craving for more. Tender ground beef, sautéed onions, and a touch of garlic come together in a symphony of flavors, all wrapped up in a delicate pierogi dough. This comforting filling pays homage to the traditional meat pierogi that has stood the test of time.

Serves Four

Ingredients:

- 1 lb ground beef

- 1 large onion, finely chopped

- 2 garlic cloves, minced

- 1 tablespoon vegetable oil

- Salt and pepper, to taste

- Pierogi dough (store-bought or homemade)

Instructions:

1. In a pan, heat the vegetable oil over medium heat. Add the chopped onions and sauté until they turn golden brown and caramelized.

2. Add the minced garlic to the pan and sauté for another minute until fragrant.

3. Add the ground beef to the pan, breaking it apart with a spatula. Cook until the beef is browned and fully cooked.

4. Season the beef mixture with salt and pepper to your liking, and allow it to cool slightly.

5. Roll out the pierogi dough and cut out circles about 3 inches in diameter.

6. Place a spoonful of the beef and onion filling in the center of each dough circle.

7. Fold the dough over the filling, forming a half-moon shape. Press the edges firmly to seal the pierogi.

8. Bring a large pot of salted water to a boil. Carefully drop the pierogi into the boiling water and cook until they float to the surface, about 2-3 minutes. Remove with a slotted spoon and set aside.

9. Serve hot with a dollop of sour cream or a side of sautéed onions for that extra touch of indulgence.

Succulent Pork and Cabbage Pierogi

Juicy ground pork meets the earthy flavors of sautéed cabbage and onions, creating a filling that's both satisfying and delicious.

Serves Four

Ingredients:

- 1 lb ground pork

- 2 cups cabbage, finely shredded

- 1 large onion, finely chopped

- 2 tablespoons butter

- Salt and pepper, to taste

- Pierogi dough (store-bought or homemade)

Instructions:

1. In a pan, melt the butter over medium heat. Add the chopped onions and sauté until they become translucent.

2. Add the finely shredded cabbage to the pan and sauté until it softens and caramelizes slightly.

3. In a separate pan, cook the ground pork until it's fully cooked and no longer pink. Drain any excess fat.

4. Combine the sautéed cabbage and onions with the cooked ground pork in a bowl. Season with salt and pepper to your liking and allow the filling to cool slightly.

5. Roll out the pierogi dough and cut out circles about 3 inches in diameter.

6. Place a spoonful of the pork and cabbage filling in the center of each dough circle.

7. Fold the dough over the filling, forming a half-moon shape. Press the edges firmly to seal the pierogi.

8. Bring a large pot of salted water to a boil. Carefully drop the pierogi into the boiling water and cook until they float to the surface, about 2-3 minutes. Remove with a slotted spoon and set aside.

9. Serve hot with a side of sour cream and a sprinkle of freshly chopped dill for a delightful Eastern European touch.

Chicken and Mushroom Pierogi

Tender chunks of chicken meet earthy mushrooms and aromatic herbs, creating a filling that's both comforting and rich in flavor. This recipe elevates pierogi to a whole new level of culinary delight!

Serves Four

Ingredients:

- 1 lb boneless, skinless chicken breast, diced

- 2 cups mushrooms, finely chopped

- 1 large onion, finely chopped

- 2 garlic cloves, minced

- 2 tablespoons butter

- 1 teaspoon dried thyme

- Salt and pepper, to taste

- Pierogi dough (store-bought or homemade)

Instructions:

1. In a pan, melt the butter over medium heat. Add the chopped onions and sauté until they become translucent.

2. Add the minced garlic to the pan and sauté for another minute until fragrant.

3. Add the diced chicken to the pan and cook until it's fully cooked and no longer pink.

4. Stir in the finely chopped mushrooms and dried thyme, sautéing until the mushrooms are tender.

5. Season the chicken and mushroom filling with salt and pepper to your liking and allow it to cool slightly.

6. Roll out the pierogi dough and cut out circles about 3 inches in diameter.

7. Place a spoonful of the chicken and mushroom filling in the center of each dough circle.

8. Fold the dough over the filling, forming a half-moon shape. Press the edges firmly to seal the pierogi.

9. Bring a large pot of salted water to a boil. Carefully drop the pierogi into the boiling water and cook until they float to the surface, about 2-3 minutes. Remove with a slotted spoon and set aside.

10. Serve hot with a side of tangy cranberry sauce or a drizzle of melted butter for a comforting meal that'll warm your soul.

Lamb and Rosemary Pierogi

This sophisticated filling combines tender ground lamb with the fragrant notes of rosemary and garlic, resulting in a truly elegant and memorable taste.

Serves Four

Ingredients:

- 1 lb ground lamb

- 2 tablespoons fresh rosemary, finely chopped

- 2 garlic cloves, minced

- 1 large onion, finely chopped

- 2 tablespoons olive oil

- Salt and pepper, to taste

- Pierogi dough (store-bought or homemade)

Instructions:

1. In a pan, heat the olive oil over medium heat. Add the chopped onions and sauté until they turn golden brown.

2. Add the minced garlic and finely chopped rosemary to the pan, sautéing until fragrant.

3. Add the ground lamb to the pan and cook until it's fully cooked and no longer pink. Season with salt and pepper to your liking.

4. Allow the lamb filling to cool slightly.

5. Roll out the pierogi dough and cut out circles about 3 inches in diameter.

6. Place a spoonful of the lamb and rosemary filling in the center of each dough circle.

7. Fold the dough over the filling, forming a half-moon shape. Press the edges firmly to seal the pierogi.

8. Bring a large pot of salted water to a boil. Carefully drop the pierogi into the boiling water and cook until they float to the surface, about 2-3 minutes. Remove with a slotted spoon and set aside.

9. Serve hot with a side of mint yogurt sauce for a refreshing complement to the rich flavors of the lamb.

Spicy Chorizo and Potato Pierogi

Get ready to ignite your taste buds with our Spicy Chorizo and Potato Pierogi! This vibrant filling brings together the fiery kick of chorizo with the comforting taste of creamy potatoes, creating a flavor fiesta in each bite.

Serves Four

Ingredients:

- 1 lb chorizo sausage, casing removed

- 2 cups potatoes, boiled and mashed

- 1 large onion, finely chopped

- 2 garlic cloves, minced

- 1 teaspoon paprika

- Salt and pepper, to taste

- Pierogi dough (store-bought or homemade)

Instructions:

1. In a pan, cook the chorizo sausage over medium heat, breaking it apart with a spatula until fully cooked and crumbled.

2. Remove the cooked chorizo from the pan and set it aside.

3. In the same pan, sauté the chopped onions and minced garlic until the onions turn translucent.

4. Add the mashed potatoes and paprika to the pan, combining them with the sautéed onions and garlic.

5. Stir in the cooked chorizo, allowing the flavors to meld together. Season with salt and pepper to your liking.

6. Roll out the pierogi dough and cut out circles about 3 inches in diameter.

7. Place a spoonful of the chorizo and potato filling in the center of each dough circle.

8. Fold the dough over the filling, forming a half-moon shape. Press the edges firmly to seal the pierogi.

9. Bring a large pot of salted water to a boil. Carefully drop the pierogi into the boiling water and cook until they float to the surface, about 2-3 minutes. Remove with a slotted spoon and set aside.

10. Serve hot with a side of tangy salsa or a dollop of sour cream to complement the bold flavors of the chorizo.

Milton Keynes UK
Ingram Content Group UK Ltd.
UKHW020645220124
436466UK00019B/830